AF585213

Australian States *and Territories*

SOUTH AUSTRALIA

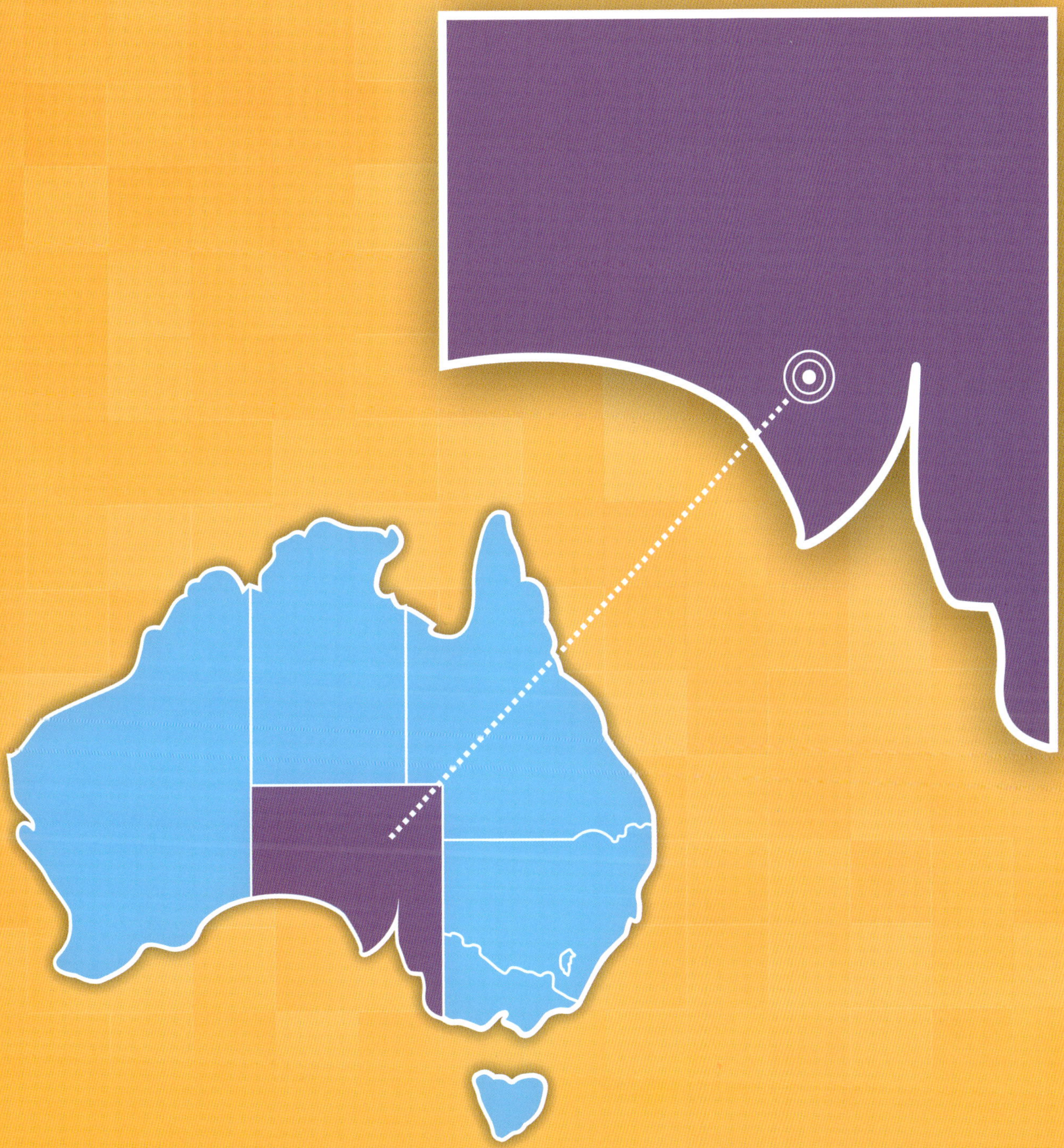

Linsie Tan

Redback Publishing
PO Box 357 Frenchs Forest NSW 2086
Australia

ISBN 978-0-9946247-4-1

First published 2017
Reprinted 2018

Author: Linsie Tan
Editor: Jane Tara
Original illustrations © Redback Publishing 2017
Originated by Redback Publishing
Printed and bound in China by Leo Paper

Acknowledgements
We would like to thank the following for permission to reproduce photographs: Mitchell Library, State Library of New South Wales, State Library of South Australia - B 7231, B 50046, B 73069/20, PRG 280/1/39/42, B 56416, Mark Marathon, Bruce Marlin, Orderinchaos, Bassano Ltd, Peter Ellis, Squiresy92.

Every effort has been made to contact copyright holders of any material reproduced in this book. Any omissions will be rectified in subsequent printings if notice is given to the publisher.

Cataloguing-in-Publication details are available from the National Library of Australia

CONTENTS

Some words are shown in red, **like this**.
You can find out what they mean by
looking in the glossary.

Geography of South Australia

South Australia is the fourth largest of Australia's states and territories. The capital city is Adelaide, located on the River Torrens. The nearest continent is Antarctica to the south.

Regions of South Australia

The Fleurieu Peninsula

The Adelaide Hills, in the Mount Lofty Ranges, form part of the Fleurieu Peninsula. The area is close to Adelaide and has wineries as well as a range of tourist attractions.

Kangaroo Island

Kangaroo Island is Australia's third largest island. It is an important sea lion sanctuary, and has a tourist industry that takes advantage of the natural beauty of the coast and the unspoiled national parks.

The Barossa Valley

Northeast of Adelaide, the Barossa Valley has been a wine producing region since the 19th century. Founded by German settlers who arrived from the late 1830s onwards, many of the local towns have a delightful German ambience. The wineries of this region produce award-winning wines with an international reputation for quality.

The Mid-North

The Mid-North is an agricultural region which also relies on tourism and light industry. The largest town is Port Pirie.

The Eyre Peninsula

The Eyre Peninsula's economy depends on agriculture and tourism. The landscape ranges from the coastline of the Great Australian Bight to the desert of the Nullarbor.

Far North

The Far North is the largest region in South Australia, and its main town is Port Augusta. Extending to the border with the Northern Territory, this region is very arid.

Limestone Coast

In the southeast of the state, the Limestone Coast is the source of a large proportion of South Australia's agricultural produce. South Australia's second largest city, Mount Gambier, is in this region.

Murray River

Paddleboats and paddlesteamers on the Murray River were once the most efficient forms of transport for local farmers moving their agricultural produce to markets in larger towns. Now the boats offer tourists an unusual style of accommodation and transport.

Great Artesian Basin

The Great Artesian Basin is a vast underground source of water. Farmers and miners drill bores into the ground, allowing the water to flow up to the surface. In dry seasons, this is the only source of water available in many communities.

Great Australian Bight

The coast of South Australia follows part of the Great Australian Bight and faces the Southern Ocean. A large marine park extends from the coast across the continental shelf.

Population

South Australia has a population of about 1.7 million people, with most of them living in Adelaide. The largest towns outside Adelaide are Mount Gambier, Gawler and Whyalla.

Deserts of South Australia

Great Victoria Desert
Strzelecki Desert
Sturt Stony Desert
Tirari Desert
Pedirka Desert

EXTREMES

- Highest recorded temperature: 50.7 °C at Oodnadatta in 1960
- Lowest recorded temperature: −8.2 °C at Yongala in 1976

FAST FACTS

Longest river
MURRAY RIVER

Highest mountain
MOUNT WOODROFFE

PREDICT THE POPULATION

Draw a graph and use it to estimate what the population will be in 2040.

YEAR	1890	1920	1950	1980	2010	2040
POPULATION of SA	166,000	245,000	365,000	652,000	808,000	?

Aboriginal History of South Australia

Aboriginal people have lived in Australia for at least 60,000 years. They developed complex societies and ways of life, and their culture depends on having strong spiritual ties to the land.

There are many different Aboriginal nations in South Australia, each with its own lands and cultural traditions. A nation is defined by its connection to its land and by its language. Groups within a nation may also have their own dialects.

European Settlers and the Aboriginal Nations

From 1838 onwards, Europeans brought cattle and sheep to South Australia, replacing the native food animals on the land. Settlers colonised areas for themselves that had been in traditional ownership for thousands of years, resulting in conflict between them and the Aboriginal people

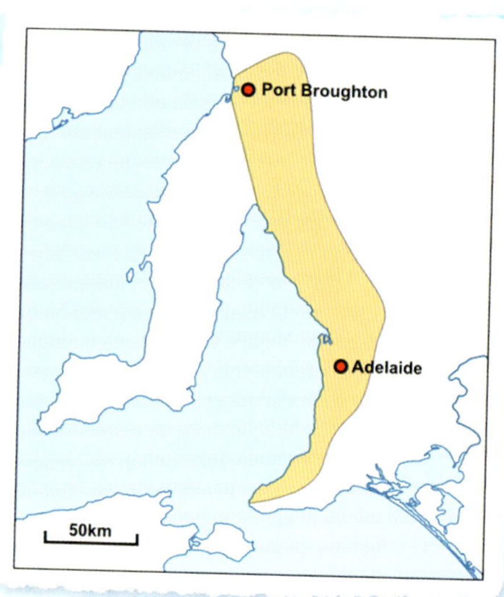

The Kaurna Nation and Language

Adelaide was founded on land belonging to the Aboriginal Kaurna nation.

In 1839, German missionaries opened a school for Aboriginal children and used the Kaurna language in their lessons. They also compiled a dictionary containing thousands of words. Some of the children's writing can be seen today in the Barr Smith Library, showing their Kaurna language written in the flowing handwriting style of the 19th century.

The Kaurna Shield

The Kaurna shield is a precious relic from over 150 years ago. It is the only known example to survive of a wokali, which is a shield used by a Kaurna man in battle. The shield was made from the bark of a red gum tree and is now kept by the South Australian Museum. The Adelaide City Council uses a symbolic drawing of it on signs in the city's parks.

FAST FACT

Aboriginal rock engravings in the Olary region of South Australia may be more than 35,000 years old.

Ngurunderi

The Dreaming story of the creation of the Murray River tells how Ngurunderi was chasing a giant Murray cod, called Ponde. Ngurunderi created the Murray River as he followed Ponde, trying to catch it.

Poonindie

In 1850, the Poonindie Settlement, near Port Lincoln, was established by the Church of England as a school for Aboriginal boys, teaching them farming techniques. The boys were placed there after being removed from their families. Poonindie operated from 1850 to 1894.

The Tjilbruke Dreaming Track

This track runs along the coastline to Rapid Bay. Visitors who follow it can find out about the history of the local Aboriginal people and the importance to them of the surrounding land and the water. Tjilbruke is one of the Kaurna creation ancestors.

Some of the many Aboriginal nations in South Australia:

Kaurna, Meru, Ngadjuri, Nawu, Banggarla, Wirangu, Kokatha, Ngarrindjeri.

How many more can you name?

WORD FILE

colonise - to settle in a new land and impose a new culture on the people living there

traditional ownership - the Aboriginal land ownership system

Ngaut Ngaut

This archaeological site near the Murray River was first studied in 1927. The rock engravings appear to show the cycles of the moon, as well as references to the sun and perhaps other astronomical symbols. The engravings are on the lands of the Ngarrindjeri nation and may be 27,000 years old.

Maralinga

In 1956, the British government was allowed to test its nuclear bombs at Maralinga, on the lands of the Maralinga Tjarutja people. Although the Aboriginal people were supposed to have all been removed from the site, the area is very remote and some remained. They later recounted how the black mist from the explosions caused them to become ill. The Maralinga land has now been returned to its traditional owners.

Colonial History of South Australia

Colonial History Timeline

17th CENTURY Dutch explorers sighted the coast of South Australia.

1802 Matthew Flinders sailed past the South Australian coast in his ship the Investigator. At the same time, French explorer Nicholas Baudin was also in the area. They both met at Encounter Bay near Victor Harbor.

1803 An American ship, whose crew was hunting seals, landed on Kangaroo Island. In the following years, sealers from various ships started an unofficial settlement on the island.

1834 The British parliament created the South Australia Act, which stated that the area was "waste and unoccupied lands" and could be claimed and colonised. The new colony was to be settled by free emigrants and not by convicts.

1835 The South Australian Company was formed in London by businessmen keen to obtain land and set up businesses in the new colony. Some of Adelaide's streets were named after the founders of this company.

8th September 1836 Surveyor William Light carved his initials into a boulder at Rapid Bay. It marked the spot where the first European officially landed in the colony of South Australia. The boulder is now in the South Australian Museum.

1836 Settlers arrived at Kangaroo Island after an eight month journey on board nine ships. Surveyor William Light was sent to the mainland to find a site for the permanent settlement.

28th September 1836 Governor Hindmarsh held a ceremony to mark the founding of South Australia.

1856 South Australia became a self-governing colony.

1872 On the completion of the Overland Telegraph Line linking Darwin and Adelaide, South Australia became the first Australian colony to be linked to London by telegraph.

1901 Federation created the state of South Australia.

Alexander Schramm. A scene in South Australia 1850

Explorers

Charles Sturt

Charles Sturt was the first European to discover the Murray River. In 1828, his expedition left New South Wales, following the Murrumbidgee River, then the Murray River, all the way to the coast. His report of land suitable for farming was one of the factors that encouraged the British government to establish the colony of South Australia. In 1846, following his return from another expedition, Sturt was able to confirm that there was no inland sea to the west.

Burke and Wills

Cooper Creek, in the Innamincka Regional Reserve, is the site where the explorers Burke and Wills died from lack of water and exhaustion. They had been the first Europeans to cross the continent from south to north and back again.

Edward John Eyre

Eyre explored the Great Australian Bight and the Nullarbor in 1840 and 1841. Travelling from Streaky Bay in South Australia to Albany in Western Australia, he managed to survive the arid conditions with the help of some Aboriginal people he encountered on the journey.

The Overland Telegraph Line

The Overland Telegraph Line was one of the construction marvels of 19th century colonial Australia. It allowed the small, isolated population of South Australia to communicate with the other colonies and the rest of the world. Beginning in Darwin in 1870, Superintendent of Telegraphs, Charles Todd, managed to construct the line to South Australia by 1872. Much of the route had not been explored, so Todd had to adapt to local engineering problems as they arose. He was given the honour of sending the first telegraph message along the line.

Transport in South Australia

Pre-Colonial Transport

The first methods of transport used by Aboriginal people in Australia were walking and paddling canoes. In South Australia, canoes were made of bark from river red gums, and they were used for fishing and to cross rivers and harbours. 'Canoe trees', which have long scars where the bark was peeled from them, are reminders of this early technology.

Aboriginal woman fishing from canoe

Settlers

The first European settlers in South Australia travelled by walking, riding horses or using coaches and carriages if they could afford them. Those living near the coast or large rivers used boats to travel locally and sailing ships to reach other parts of colonial Australia.

Two Afghan cameleers, 1905

Camels

Settlers in the desert areas of South Australia relied on camels for the delivery of freight to their isolated settlements. Afghan cameleers operated these camel delivery services during the 19th century. Camels were also used to carry equipment and building materials for the Overland Telegraph Line and South Australia's explorers used them on their pioneering journeys across the deserts.

Cobb & Co Coaches

A stage coach service operated by Cobb & Co in the mid to late 1800s carried mail and passengers to towns in rural South Australia. Horses had to be changed at staging posts along the way, and the provision of feed and water for them was always a consideration when the stage coach was travelling to any remote area.

TIME TRAVELLER

Imagine you are a passenger on a Cobb & Co coach in 1870. What can you see out the window? How do you feel after the long, bumpy journey?

Roads

Roads in colonial South Australia were not good enough to provide reliable transport for colonial farmers, loggers and miners needing to get their produce to ports on the coast. Trains on land and paddlesteamers on the Murray River took over this role. Once the goods reached the ports, export to other parts of Australia and overseas relied on ships.

Shipping Ports

The South Australian government privatised its ports in 2001. Facilities are provided for freight and cruise shipping.

- Port Adelaide
- Port Pirie
- Port Lincoln
- Port Giles
- Klein Point
- Thevenard
- Wallaroo

Smaller port towns around the coast developed to provide shipping services for settlers before the use of large ports and containers ships. These small port towns still provide harbours and facilities for fishing vessels, tourism, pleasure boating and whale-watching businesses.

Air Transport

Airports in South Australia include:

- Adelaide International Airport
- Regional airports
- Military airstrips
- Private landing strips on farms and mining areas

Trams

South Australia's first tram service was horse-drawn and operated from 1855, between Port Elliot and Goolwa. In Adelaide, horse-drawn trams operated from 1878 right up until 1914, when electric trams replaced them. The tram to Glenelg is the only service now operating.

The last horse tram to Burnside, 1909

Steam train South Australia 1920

Railways

A railway line for steam trains began operating between Adelaide and Port Adelaide in 1856. The need for a railway service to transport mining and agricultural produce resulted in a line to Kapunda being opened in 1860. Other lines were opened from the interior to ports on the coast, but they were not linked to each other until the 1880s. The narrow width of these early lines made them cheaper to construct. The last steam engine service in South Australia ran in 1970.

Kati Thanda - Lake Eyre

Lake Eyre's Aboriginal name is Kati Thanda. It is 700 kilometres north of Adelaide and is the lowest point in Australia, at about 15 metres below sea level. Kati Thanda - Lake Eyre is on the lands of the Arabana Aboriginal nation.

The Arabana people ask that visitors do not walk on the lake out of respect for its spiritual significance.

Kati Thanda - Lake Eyre is Australia's largest salt lake, measuring 144 kilometres long by 77 kilometres wide. It periodically fills with water which then evaporates to leave a salty crust. The amount of water in the lake depends on the monsoon. As the lake fills, thousands of waterbirds migrate to it. They include birds that are normally only seen in seaside locations, such as pelicans, gulls and terns. The birds feed on insects and on the small fish that multiply in the lake.

Surrounding Kati Thanda are red sand dunes, flat topped tablelands and a stone covered desert. In summer the temperature is very high, causing the lake water to evaporate.

Tourism to Kati Thanda

Kati Thanda is in a national park and visitors must abide by regulations for their own safety and for the benefit of the local environment.

- The area is very remote and can only be accessed by 4WD vehicles.
- There is no mobile phone coverage so visitors need to be aware of their own safety.
- Tourists should travel in convoys and need to carry all their own vehicle spare parts, fuel, water and food.
- Travel is not recommended during the hottest months from November to March.
- There are basic campsites in the national park.
- Pets are not allowed.
- Travellers should not drive on the salt crust as it is thin and brittle.
- Campfires must be extinguished with water, not with sand.
- Collection of wood for fires is prohibited in the national park.

Why are no pets allowed in the Kati Thanda area?

WORD FILE

convoy - a group of vehicles travelling together

Rules for Outback Travel

Look at each of these rules and think about why they exist.

- Do not leave your vehicle if it breaks down.
- Check road conditions at the nearest town before starting the journey.
- Stay on the roads and do not drive off-road.
- Take note of road closure signs.
- Take your rubbish away with you.

Plant and Animal Adaptations to the Salt Lake Habitat

Plants

The salt lake is surrounded by sparse desert vegetation. When the lake is dry, plants near it include mulga, acacias and tussocks of long grasses. All of these plants are drought tolerant.

When the lake is full of fresh water, there is an explosion of growth surrounding it. Many of these plants have to grow and produce seeds quickly, before the water dries up. They attract birds and insects to pollinate them and disperse their seeds. These seeds will then have to be dormant during the dry months when the lake turns into salt crystals.

Animals

The Lake Eyre dragon is a lizard that has adapted to live on the dry lake. It uses the salt crust as a shelter and feeds on ants.

As the water of Kati Thanda - Lake Eyre evaporates it becomes more and more salty. The Lake Eyre hardyhead fish has adapted to these conditions and can live in water up to 15 times saltier than seawater. Other life in the lake waters includes bream, perch and shrimp.

Migratory birds survive by leaving when the water dries up. Some of them travel all the way back to China and Japan as part of their migration flights.

Industries in South Australia

Wineries

The Barossa Valley has been producing fine wines since German settlers arrived there in the mid 1800s. Many of the larger wineries are household names around Australia, and their products are exported throughout the world.

The wine making regions of South Australia are:

- Adelaide Hills
- Barossa Valley
- Clare Valley
- Coonawarra
- Eden Valley
- Langhorne Creek
- McLaren Vale
- Padthaway

Mining Facts

- The world's largest lead and silver smelter is located at Port Pirie and it has been in operation for over 120 years.
- Opal is mined at Andamooka and Coober Pedy.
- South Australia has the largest uranium deposit in the world, and mines 23 per cent of the world's uranium.
- Coal is mined at Leigh Creek and is used to generate electricity.
- Copper mining contributed to the development of South Australia from the 1840s. The state has 68 per cent of Australia's copper resources.
- The Olympic Dam deposits of copper, uranium, gold and silver are a remarkably large collection of ores and one of the largest known to exist anywhere.
- In 1915, the town of Iron Knob became the birthplace of iron mining in Australia.
- The Eyre Peninsula has reserves of graphite that can be mined for use in the energy industry.

FAST FACTS

What makes uranium mining different?

- The Australian government imposes controls on who can buy uranium
- Any buyer must only use Australian mining for peaceful purposes
- The radioactive mining waste needs special disposal methods

Tourism

South Australia is known as the Festival State. Many events featuring artists, writers and performers are held throughout the year and attract thousands of tourists.

The national parks, coastline, historic locations and rivers make South Australia a favoured destination for visitors. The influence of the German settlers is seen in many small villages, whose European style buildings and Lutheran churches have created a little piece of Germany in the heart of South Australia.

Wine tourism is very important in South Australia. Visitors to the wine regions sample fine wines and also enjoy seeing how they are made.

Woomera

The Woomera Prohibited Area is a restricted region used for national defence and security purposes. From 1942 to 1982, the Woomera Rocket Range operated in the area. It was the location of weapons testing and rocket launches.

The land around Woomera has significant deposits of gold, iron ore and other minerals.

Whaling and Sealing

Whaling and sealing were the first large industries in South Australia. Ships operated in the waters around the Eyre Peninsula even before the colony of South Australia was founded. A small, unofficial settlement of whalers and sealers existed on Kangaroo Island in 1803.

The whale oil was used for lighting and on machinery, while the whale bones were used to make women's corsets. Seal fur and whale products were exported from South Australia and sold around the world. Whaling in South Australia eventually became unprofitable as petroleum products and plastics replaced the whale products in consumer goods.

Petroleum Industry

Petroleum and natural gas are produced in northeast South Australia from the Cooper and Eromanga Basins, which are the largest onshore petroleum areas in Australia. Natural gas was first discovered in the Cooper Basin in the 1960s. The products are processed at Moomba and gas is then piped to consumers.

WORD FILE

smelter - a factory which extracts metal from ore

Agriculture in South Australia

The first European explorers of South Australia reported back to the governments of Britain and New South Wales that the areas they found would provide good pastures for livestock and land for growing crops. Agriculture was an important industry in the new colony right from its beginnings.

Commercial Fishing

Commercial fishing throughout South Australia is regulated, and there are fines for taking protected species. Fish that are protected from commercial fishing in South Australia include both freshwater and marine species. Some of these are wild Murray cod, white sharks, abalone and yabbies. All marine mammals are protected in every location and in all seasons.

Aquaculture

Aquaculture is the raising of aquatic food animals in ponds, tanks or in enclosures in the ocean. Aquaculture in South Australia produces a range of foods, including trout, tuna, oysters, barramundi, abalone, Murray cod and yabbies.

Crops

Crops grown in South Australia include wheat, barley, oats, rye, triticale, peas, beans, lentils, canola and hay. South Australia places strict controls on the growing of any GM crops, and non-GM canola from South Australia is marketed to consumers looking for a natural alternative.

WHAT IS GM FOOD?

GM stands for 'genetically modified'. GM foods have been altered by scientists using gene technology.

Horticulture

Farmers in South Australia grow vegetables, fruits and nuts. Some of the areas growing this produce are:
The Adelaide Hills - apples, pears, cherries and strawberries
The Adelaide Plains - tomatoes, capsicums and cucumbers
The Riverland - fruit and almonds

South Australia does not have fruit flies. To protect its horticulture, the state has strict quarantine regulations restricting the import of fruits and vegetables, which could be harbouring this pest.

Livestock

Cattle, sheep and pigs are the main livestock raised in South Australia. Owners of livestock pay a fee to the government based on the number of animals they own. These funds are used to control diseases, maintain the Dog Fence and administer the industry.

The Dog Fence was first built in the 1880s to protect livestock in the south of Australia from attacks by dingoes and wild dogs. The fence runs from Queensland across to South Australia and ends at the Eyre Peninsula.

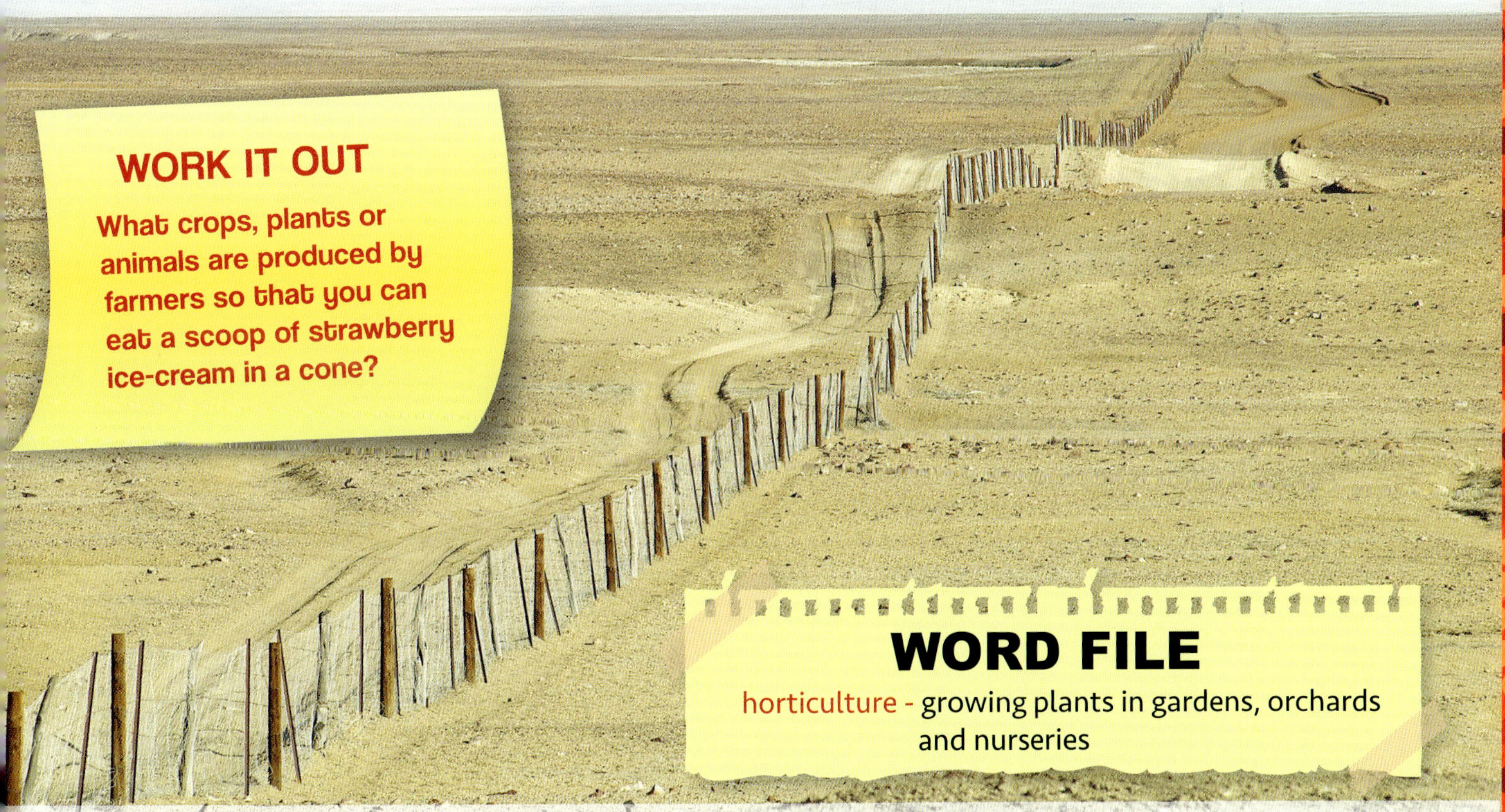

WORK IT OUT

What crops, plants or animals are produced by farmers so that you can eat a scoop of strawberry ice-cream in a cone?

WORD FILE

horticulture - growing plants in gardens, orchards and nurseries

Forestry

All the timber logged in South Australia comes from plantations. The native forests are not harvested. Wood products include timber for building and furniture, pulp for papermaking, and wood for domestic heating.

Wine

Half of all the vineyards in Australia are located in South Australia, which produces 80 per cent of the country's fine wines. Exports are sent to many countries, with the main customers being in China, the UK, the USA and Canada.

Environment and Sustainability in South Australia

Sustainable practices require a balance between using the land and waterways for development and keeping areas as regions of natural beauty.

Protecting Native Plants and Animals

South Australia lists 324 threatened animal species. These include:

- 100 mammal species
- 163 bird species
- 53 reptile species
- 8 amphibian species

There are 828 plant species listed as threatened or extinct.

RESOURCES	HOW WE CAN LOOK AFTER THEM
SOIL	Correct use of fertilisers and avoiding soil erosion
WATER	Keeping water supplies unpolluted
NATIVE PLANTS	Avoid complete clearing of areas for pastures
NATIVE ANIMALS	Keep some areas of natural bushland for food and shelter
AIR QUALITY	Avoid polluting the air through poor industrial practices

Energy Production

Electricity in South Australia is generated from natural gas, coal, wind energy and solar cells.

Natural gas - South Australia's natural gas comes locally from Moomba and Katnook, as well as from plants in Victoria and Queensland.
Wind energy - South Australia is the largest producer of wind energy in Australia.
Solar cells - South Australia was the first state in Australia to encourage residents to install solar power.
Coal - The Leigh Creek coalfield, approximately 260 kilometres north of Port Augusta, is the most productive open-cut coalfield in the world.

The South Australian government is committed to reducing greenhouse gas emissions and increasing the use of renewable energy sources.

Leigh Creek coalfield

Water

South Australia is a very dry state. As well as using water from reservoirs, South Australia also needs to use recycled and desalinated water sources. Desalinated water has had the salt removed. The three desalination plants in South Australia are on Kangaroo Island, at Hawker in the Flinders Ranges and at Port Stanvac.

Desalination tower at Beresford Siding, Oodnadatta Track, South Australia

Murray River Salinity

Increasing salinity in the Murray River causes problems for the environment and for users of the water.

- Salty water cannot be used for drinking.
- Salty irrigation water will damage or kill crops.
- As water evaporates from farmlands it leaves salt in the soil, making the land unusable for planting crops.
- High salt levels in water drawn from the Murray River will cause corrosion of pipes and fittings.

Biosecurity

South Australia restricts the import of some fruit and vegetables. Soil is also a prohibited import. Quarantine stations exist throughout the state to check that diseased and pest-infested plants and animals are not being brought into the state. The health and viability of South Australia's agriculture depend on the enforcement of its quarantine rules. Kangaroo Island places additional restrictions on bees, honey and potatoes to protect its own agriculture.

WORD FILE

biosecurity - controlling plants, insects and animals that are harmful

PESKY PESTS

These animals are considered pests in South Australia:

feral camels, feral deer, feral foxes, feral goats, feral pigs, mice, wild dogs and dingoes, wild rabbits.

Government of South Australia

No convicts were sent to South Australia. The colonists were all free immigrants who believed they should have an independent and elected government. Their belief in their right to be allowed to vote for their parliament led to South Australia becoming an early leader in a number of electoral reforms.

South Australian Government Timeline

60,000 years ago Aboriginal nations governed according to their own laws.

1836 Governor Hindmarsh established the new colony of South Australia. Power to run the colony was divided between the Governor and the Resident Commissioner, James Fisher.

Governor Hindmarsh

1857 South Australia gained its own bicameral parliament with a House of Assembly (Lower House) and a Legislative Council (Upper House). All adult males over the age of 21 years old could vote for members of the Lower House, but voters for the Upper House had to own or lease property of a set value. In theory, these voting rights also included Aboriginal men.

1863 - 1901 The Northern Territory was added to South Australia as the electorate of Flinders.

1890s The first political parties were formed and became the forerunners of the Liberal Party and the Australian Labor Party in South Australia.

1894 South Australia became the first place in Australia to allow women to vote and to stand for election to parliament.

1901 Federation created the state of South Australia.

1962 Aboriginal people had the right to vote in Federal elections.

1972 The voting age was lowered to 18 years old.

1973 Voters for the Upper House no longer had to be landowners.

FAST FACT

'Terra nullius' is Latin for 'land that nobody owns'. The British government used this idea to allow it to claim land in South Australia.

The Suffragettes

The Women's Suffrage League was formed in Adelaide in 1888 and worked tirelessly to gain votes for women. In 1914, Adela Pankhurst, daughter of the famous British suffragette, Emmeline Pankhurst, spoke in Adelaide and praised the local women's movement. South Australia had already achieved the voting rights that her mother was still campaigning for in Britain.

Mary Lee, 1821-1909, Secretary of the Women's Suffrage League, 1888-1894

Votes for Aboriginal Women

In 1894, a number of Aboriginal women from the Ngarrindjeri mission at Point McLeay insisted on enrolling to vote, against the wishes of the mission manager. More than 70 of them recorded their vote at the next elections.

Parliament House

South Australia's first parliament house was opened in 1843. A much larger and grander building was built in 1889, using marble from Kapunda and granite from West Island. The east wing of the building was completed in 1939.

Local Government

There are 68 local councils in South Australia. They are responsible for local roads, rubbish collection, libraries, parks and sports facilities.

The Adelaide City Council was established in 1840, making it the oldest local government in Australia. The first mayor was James Fisher.

WORD FILE

bicameral - a government having two houses or sections

The South Australian Parliament Today

The House of Assembly (Upper House) has 47 members.
The Legislative Council (Lower House) has 22 members.

The Governor of South Australia is nominated by the state government and appointed by the Queen.

Opening of Parliament House, by the Governor-General, 5th June 1939

Notable People from South Australia

Jubilee 150 Walk

In 1986, a group of 150 plaques was installed along the footpath on the north side of North Terrace in Adelaide. The plaques commemorate famous South Australians. Look out for them the next time you visit Adelaide.

Howard Florey (1898 - 1968) Howard Florey was born in Adelaide. In 1945, he was awarded a Nobel Prize for the discovery of penicillin, a life-saving antibiotic. In 1965, he was honoured by the Queen, who made him Lord Florey. He also became Chancellor of the Australian National University.

Roma Mitchell (1913 - 2000) Roma Mitchell was born in Adelaide. She was the first woman to be appointed to a number of official positions, including Justice of the Supreme Court, Governor of South Australia and Chancellor of the University of Adelaide. She was awarded the OBE in 1971 and, just before her death, she was honoured with a Royal Victorian Order.

Greg Chappell (1948 -) Greg Chappell was born in Unley. He captained the Australian cricket team from 1975 to 1977, as well as from 1979 until his retirement from competitive sport in 1984. As a player in the controversial World Series Cricket competition, Greg Chappell achieved outstanding results. He has also been a selector, a coach and a member of the Australian Cricket Board.

Gladys Elphick (1904 - 1988) Gladys Elphick was a Narannga woman whose work for the Aboriginal community resulted in her receiving many awards, including an MBE in 1971. Known as Aunty Glad, she was responsible for founding the Aboriginal Women's Council in 1965 and became a member of the State Aboriginal Affairs Board in the same year. The Gladys Elphick Awards are held each year to recognise the work of Aboriginal women in South Australia and to build on Aunty Glad's legacy.

Doris Graham Doris Graham was a Kaurna Elder whose work for reconciliation is commemorated by the Doris Graham Commemorative Plaque in Elder Park, near the Festival Centre in Adelaide. For some years Doris Graham was the oldest woman in Adelaide. In 1997, she signed Adelaide City Council's Reconciliation Vision Statement.

Make Your Own List

What makes a person memorable? Who are three people you think are memorable in your family, school or suburb?

Marcus Oliphant (1901 – 2000) Marcus Oliphant was born in Adelaide. He was a noted scientist whose work on nuclear physics contributed to the development of atomic weapons. In his later years, he condemned the use of atomic energy for destructive purposes. He was a founder of the Australian Academy of Science in 1954, was knighted in 1959 and was Governor of South Australia in the 1970s.

Sidney Kidman (1857 - 1935) Sidney Kidman was born at Athelstone. Starting his working life as a drover, he began to build his wealth by expanding into transport and butcher shops. Kidman eventually bought cattle properties and created a cattle station empire covering an area larger than Tasmania. He was knighted for his exceptional contribution to industry in Australia.

Douglas Nicholls (1906 - 1988) Douglas Nicholls was a successful Australian Rules football player and coach, but his most high profile appointment was as Governor of South Australia in 1976. As a Church of Christ minister he worked in Fitzroy doing welfare work and preaching, and became one of the founders of NAIDOC Week. He worked tirelessly for Indigenous rights and for reconciliation, and in recognition of this received a knighthood, an MBE and an OBE. Sir Douglas was a Yorta Yorta man.

David Unaipon (1872 - 1967) David Unaipon was born at the Point McLeay Mission. A Yaraldi man, he patented many inventions, including a shearing tool and a centrifugal motor. He was nicknamed Australia's Leonardo because of the broad range of his interests and skills. For fifty years he travelled and preached religion as well as speaking about his inventions and about Aboriginal legends. He wrote articles about these legends for newspapers and also wrote books and poetry on these subjects. As an unofficial spokesman for Indigenous people in the 1920s, David Unaipon made suggestions to governments and even believed in the establishment of a separate Aboriginal territory in Australia. His picture is on Australia's fifty-dollar note.

Colin Thiele (1920 - 2006) Colin Thiele was born in Eudunda and was a popular children's book author. His stories were often set in the South Australian rural areas of his childhood. His most well-known novel is Storm Boy, about a friendship between a boy and an injured pelican. The story was made into a movie in 1976. Colin Thiele was also a teacher and school Principal.

Immigration to South Australia

60,000 Years Ago

The ancestors of the Australian Aboriginal people arrived from the north and spread throughout the country. The northern parts of Australia were connected to other landmasses 8,000 years ago, when the sea levels were lower than they are today, and people could travel easily across the shallow seas.

TIME TRAVELLER, 1913

Imagine you are a 14-year old Barwell Boy who has just arrived in Adelaide from Britain. What are your thoughts on your first night in South Australia? How do you feel about the weather, the open spaces and being so far away from home?

Britain

In 1834, the British parliament created the South Australia Act, which stated that the area was "waste and unoccupied lands" and could be claimed and colonised. The same act set up an Emigration Fund to send the poor from Ireland and Great Britain to the new colony, provided they were *"adult persons of the two sexes in equal proportions, And not exceeding the age of thirty years."* The first settlers arrived in 1836 on board nine ships.

When copper deposits were discovered in Burra in 1845, miners from Cornwall, Wales, England and Scotland came to the area and helped to create one of the world's largest tin mines.

In 1913, the first group of Barwell Boys arrived from England. They were part of a South Australian scheme to bring teenage boys to the state and train them as farm apprentices to help ease the labour shortage. Soon after arrival, the boys were assigned to farmers in rural South Australia and started work in conditions that were completely different from what they were used to

Large group of 'Barwell Boys'

Germany

By 1900, German settlers and their descendants made up about 10 per cent of South Australia's population. Most of them took up farming and viticulture, but some settled in Adelaide and opened businesses. The German Lutherans were escaping religious persecution in their own country, and were attracted to South Australia because it had a policy right from the beginning making all religions equal.

Klemzig, the first German settlement in Australia (now a suburb of Adelaide), painted by George French Angas in 1846

Asia

In 1857, the gold rush in Victoria resulted in 15,000 Chinese arriving in South Australia. To avoid paying the tax on Chinese people who arrived at ports in Victoria, the Chinese gold miners landed at ports on the South Australian coast, then walked overland to the Victorian gold fields.

In the 1970s, following the Vietnam War, many Vietnamese refugees settled in Adelaide. The Vietnamese and Cambodian migrants became prominent in horticulture and now supply much of Adelaide's fresh produce.

Middle East

The Afghan cameleers worked throughout South Australia in the mid to late 1800s, providing a freight service to many remote towns in desert areas. Their camels were suited to the arid conditions, and the Afghans provided a vital source of supply for a range of consumer goods. They also transported building materials to desert areas.

There are many people who have come from countries around the world to settle in South Australia. How many of these countries can you name?

Although the locals called them all Afghans, many of the men were also from Pakistan and Northern India. Some eventually returned home to their own country, while others stayed and raised families in Australia. The building of the mosque in Little Gilbert Street, Adelaide, was financed by a group of Afghan cameleers who wanted a permanent place where they could go to attend services.

The Darwin to Adelaide train, The Ghan, is named after the Afghan cameleers.

Romani Gypsies

In the 1990s, the South Australian headquarters of Romani International Australia was located in Adelaide. At that time there were about 20,000 Romani people in Australia.

After 1945

After the Second World War, migrants and war refugees came to South Australia from many countries in Europe, including Italy, Greece, The Netherlands, Germany, eastern Europe and Britain. Hostels for the new arrivals were located at Woodside in the Adelaide Hills and at Pennington in the Adelaide suburbs.

Major Sites in South Australia

These sites include buildings, structures and natural features. They are important for their beauty, their rarity and their historic connections.

Fossil Caves at Naracoorte

The fossil caves in the Naracoorte Caves National Park are World Heritage listed. They are amongst the world's ten most important fossil sites, and contain remains that reveal the evolutionary history of Australia's unique and isolated animals. Some of the fossils date back over 350,000 years and include ice-age megafauna.

At the Wonambi Fossil Centre, visitors can look at scenes that have been created to show the animals and how they would have looked in their ancient environments.

Adelaide Festival Centre

The Adelaide Festival Centre was designed by John Morphett and opened in1973. It hosts opera, concerts and drama and is South Australia's centre for the performing arts.

Adelaide Gaol

The Adelaide Gaol was used from 1841 - 1988. It is one of the two oldest public buildings in Adelaide. Visitors can take tours of the site and find out about the way prisoners lived and were treated in the earliest days of the colony. The gaol has a reputation for being the most haunted place in South Australia.

Carrick Hill

Carrick Hill is a rare surviving example of a 20th century mansion with most of its contents, decor and gardens still intact. It was once the home of Sir Edward and Lady Ursula Hayward, and is now a museum that is open to the public.

Flinders Ranges

The landscape of the Flinders Ranges is up to 540 million years old. The countryside ranges from forests to deserts, and includes gorges and mountains. There are many national parks across the Flinders Ranges with walking trails where tourists can get close to nature. The Cullyamurra Waterhole is said to be Australia's largest billabong and it attracts an array of wildlife.

Adelaide Botanic Garden

First opened in 1857, the Adelaide Botanic Garden has a number of historic buildings:

- Palm House - 1877
- Santos Museum of Economic Botany - 1879
- Goodman Building - 1909

Modern additions to the Botanic Garden include the Rose Garden (1996) and the Bicentennial Conservatory (1989), which is the largest single span conservatory in the southern hemisphere.

Flags, Symbols, Emblems and Special Days of South Australia

People living in South Australia use flags, symbols and special days to show their connection to their community. These connections include pride for the group they belong to, an interest in the history of their group or area, and wanting to join others for celebrations that bring people together.

South Australian State Flag

The state flag was officially proclaimed in 1904. The Union Jack on the flag is a reminder of South Australia's historic ties with Britain. The badge shows the piping shrike, a bird of the open forests of South Australia. It sits on a gumtree branch and behind it is a golden circle, representing the rising sun.

Australian Aboriginal Flag

The Aboriginal flag was first flown in Victoria Square, Adelaide, on 9th July 1971 as a symbol supporting the land rights movement. The flag was designed by Elder Harold Thomas.

Yellow disc - the sun and yellow ochre
Red - the land
Black - the Aboriginal people of Australia

Special Days

Australia Day - On 26th January each year, Australians commemorate the 1788 founding of a British colony by Governor Phillip at Sydney Cove.
ANZAC Day - Ceremonies and marches for ANZAC Day are held all around the state on 25th April each year.
NAIDOC Week - A week in July each year to celebrate the history, culture and achievements of Aboriginal and Torres Strait Islander peoples. Communities and government bodies organise events around the state for NAIDOC Week.

RULES FOR FLYING THESE FLAGS

- Don't fly more than one on the same pole.
- Don't fly them in the dark.
- Raise the flag to the top of the pole before lowering it to half-mast.
- Treat these flags with respect.

Holidays only held in South Australia

Proclamation Day in December is a holiday celebrating the establishment of the colony of South Australia in 1836. This date is the Boxing Day holiday in other states.
The March Public Holiday coincides with the Adelaide Cup horse race.

Symbols of South Australia

Floral Emblem - Sturt's desert pea
Animal Emblem - Hairy nosed wombat
Gemstone emblem - Opal
Marine Emblem - Leafy sea dragon

The Coat of Arms

Each part of the Coat of Arms has a meaning:

Piping shrike - a South Australian bird
Sturt's desert pea - the state flower
Wheat, barley and fruit - represent agriculture
Cog wheels - represent industry
Miner's pick - represents mining

Unlike the other Australian states, South Australia's coat of arms does not include a Latin motto.

WORD FILE

Elder - a respected Aboriginal person who is a custodian of traditional knowledge
half-mast - flying a flag halfway up the pole as a mark of respect when a community leader dies

Make Your Own Coat of Arms

Design a Coat of Arms for your family, suburb or sport group, etc.

- Use symbols that everyone will know
- Your own Coat of Arms could include drawings or pictures to tell the history of the group
- Think about where to use your Coat of Arms
- What language will you use for a motto?
- Where have you seen the SA Coat of Arms used?

How to Find Out More
Primary and Secondary Sources

There are many ways to find out more about South Australia. You can do this using both primary and secondary sources. Websites can have a mixture of both types of sources on them.

Primary Sources

- **Interviews** - when people say what they have seen
- **Letters** - when the writer was the person experiencing the event
- **Newspapers** - when the facts are presented such as a list of prices for groceries
- **Photos** - when they have not been altered
- **Maps**
- **Old Items & Antiques**
- **News on Television** - when it shows pictures of real events
- **School Newsletters** - when they list names or dates of events
- **Videos on Youtube or Facebook** - when they show an event and have not been altered

Secondary Sources

- **Letters** - when the writer is retelling the facts that someone else told them
- **Newspapers** - when the story is told by someone who retells the facts that someone else told them
- **Photos** - when the photo has been altered
- **Songs, Poems, Stories**
- **News on Television** - when it is reported by a journalist who did not experience the events

The
FRIDAY EVENING, DECEMBER 8, 1939
On West Front
FINLAN
REPEL ENEMY
ALONG WHOLE
ESTERN FRONT
s Crumble Before
And Infantry
PARIS, Thursday.
a quickening of activities along
s from German patrols
intense fire, started en-
y fire and infantry
ther has led
The
and

Fun Activities Using Sources

- Find old newspapers at your local library. Use these to look at pictures of areas you know and see how they have changed over time.
- Take photos of your school, paste them into an exercise book, add some notes and ask the librarian to add your book to the collection. This will then become a primary source for students in the future.
- Ask students and teachers to tell you what they know about the history of your school. Type the results into a Word document, print it and staple the pages into a booklet. You now have a secondary source for people to use in the future. Ask the librarian to add your booklet to the library collection.
- See if your town or school has been mentioned in parliament by searching its name in the Hansard record. Go to http://hansardpublic.parliament.sa.gov.au

South Australian Museum

WORD FILE

Hansard - a record of what the politicians say in parliament

Your Own Family and Friends

Primary sources do not always have to be about famous people. Interviews with your family and friends are important too. Your grandmother might recall what your suburb used to be like. Friends can share stories about coming to live in South Australia either from other states or from a country overseas.

Museums in South Australia

South Australian Museum, Adelaide
Tramway Museum, Adelaide
South Australian Maritime Museum, Port Adelaide
National Railway Museum, Port Adelaide
National Motor Museum, Birdwood
Migration Museum, Adelaide

Websites

Find more information about South Australia on these websites:

- www.sa.gov.au
- www.parliament.sa.gov.au
- www.pir.sa.gov.au
- www.sahistoryhub.com.au

Glossary

bicameral - a government having two houses or sections
biosecurity - controlling plants, insects and animals that are harmful
colonise - to settle in a new land and impose a new culture on the people living there
convoy - a group of vehicles travelling together
Elder - a respected Aboriginal person who is a custodian of traditional knowledge
half-mast - flying a flag halfway up the pole as a mark of respect when a community leader dies
Hansard - a record of what the politicians say in parliament
horticulture - growing plants in gardens, orchards and nurseries
smelter - a factory which extracts metal from ore
traditional ownership - the Aboriginal land ownership system in existence before the arrival of Europeans

Index

www.redbackpublishing.com.au